GOLF
IS
GOD'S GAME

GOLF
IS
GOD'S GAME

◆

GOLF FROM A BIBLICAL
PERSPECTIVE

TONY M. SMALL

iUniverse, Inc.
New York Lincoln Shanghai

Golf is God's Game
Golf from a Biblical Perspective

iUniverse books may be ordered through booksellers or by contacting:

iUniverse
2021 Pine Lake Road, Suite 100
Lincoln, NE 68512
www.iuniverse.com
1-800-Authors (1-800-288-4677)

ISBN-13: 978-0-595-38677-2 (pbk)
ISBN-13: 978-0-595-83060-2 (ebk)
ISBN-10: 0-595-38677-6 (pbk)
ISBN-10: 0-595-83060-9 (ebk)

Printed in the United States of America

This book is dedicated to:

My mom and dad, who taught me to love the game and learn about myself, and then improve.

To Don Pohl, who told me to "do it!" Someone once said, "Everyone has one good book in his or her mind.

You have one, too!"

AND...

My belief that "golf is God's game."

For God so loved the world that he gave his only son that whoever believes in him will not perish but have everlasting life.

—(John 3:16)

Then he gave us the game of golf to enjoy while we are on earth…so that we might learn more about ourselves, the people we deal with and the world we live in.

CONTENTS

INTRODUCTION

You are about to embark on an enlightening trip through what the author calls an airplane book: a manuscript easily read in one short trip of an hour and a half or less.

This book is intended to give the reader a new perspective on golf. It will not give you the nuts and bolts of the golf swing. It will, however, give you insight into a better golf game, by improving your mental and emotional approach to the game.

Using the Bible as a baseline, the author intends to give you a perspective that will help you improve both yourself and your game through proper mental management of your game.

This book will help you with your game quickly while improving your personal knowledge of your inner self. Controlling your emotions while golfing will lower your score even if your physical game is not at its very best on any given day.

1

MY INTRODUCTION TO THE GAME

I will always remember my unique introduction to this glorious game. Actually, I was introduced to the golf course even before I learned how to play the game. At the age of seven, I was given the option of going to the course with my mom and dad or sitting at home with my teenage siblings. Since choosing to stay home would afford me the opportunity to sit on my hands while we watched their favorite shows on black-and-white television, I chose the fresh air and open spaces of the golf course.

At Pine Hills Golf Club, just outside Ottawa, Illinois, I would run the fairways, chase the squirrels, and drink water from the old hand pump properly placed in the middle of the course. My mom and dad would rent one of those indestructible two-wheel hand-carts, the kind that carries one bag plus anything else you want.

When my parents had a tee time, I came along simply for the fun of it. I had the run of the golf course. After several holes, I would be exhausted. My dad would let me ride on the cart, with his clubs, and pull me all the way back to the clubhouse. I would usually fall asleep before we left the course and then sleep all the way home. Once in the house, I was down for the count, out for the night. My parents obviously had their child-management skills in high gear—after all, I was the youngest of five.

As I ran through those years with my friend Jim, we discovered every corner of the course, from the creek beds to golf balls in the woods, even building forts when we had nothing better to do. We still, to this day, talk about those times and the carefree youth we enjoyed.

Later, because I'm left-handed, my dad found a couple of left-handed clubs for me that I couldn't swing. Eventually, I discovered right-handed clubs, which felt much better to me. I could hit them a New York City mile. Later in life I would discover that I was right-eyed. I believe this is the reason why right-handed clubs worked for me.

I look back on those great years with wonder at the wisdom my parents showed by allowing me to fall in love with the game rather than forcing it on me by making me go with them. Over time, I learned to enjoy the game. My dad would let me play until I lost interest, and then I would "ride the cart" until the round was over. As the years progressed, I wanted to play more and more with him, and my dad gave me the okay. His only request was that I simply keep up with the pace of play. And I would try. When I couldn't, I rode the cart to catch up; then I could play some more. On a small course like the one I grew up on, everyone knew each other, so it was easy to enjoy the time together.

I would recommend you use this method to introduce golf to your child. Allow your child to tag along and simply enjoy your God-given time together with NO requirements of performance. Always allow your children to grow into the game rather than forcing the game on them.

2
FRUITS OF
THE GAME

But the fruit of the spirit is love, joy, peace, patience, kindness, goodness, faithfulness, gentleness, self-control; against such there is no law.

—(Gal 5:22–23)

Few people embody these attributes and thus are truly "full of His Spirit." Successful golfers will tell you that most of these qualities are necessary to play the game at the highest level.

So, let's look at the fruit of the Spirit in detail. Each piece of fruit is an essential component that wills the player to grow his or her understanding of the game.

LOVE

Most people who play the game will, after a period of time, either fall in love with it or leave it, never to return. Those of us who do love it dearly play the game regularly with a passion that few can understand, and we can never get enough, no matter what the weather.

Many wives call themselves "golf widows." Some do so in jest and some in earnest, but all will tell you their husbands are refreshed when they return from the course. My wife learned of my love for the game early on. She has often said, "You need to go play; you haven't in a while." Although I may not play well, just being out on the course rejuvenates me greatly and allows me to return to the world with a fresh attitude.

I would like to tell all the golf widows to take up the game. This will increase your time with the man you love and add to your exercise regimen, and you'll enjoy a great game. You might also have fun bringing the kids with you and making it a family affair. Whether you play the game, hit balls at the driving range, or just watch people play from the golf course's patio, this event can become a great family outing with little expense. Give it a try; you might just enjoy it immensely.

JOY

In the Beginning: The Joy of Youth

Any child interested in playing the great game of golf should have the experience of simply hitting a golf ball for the first time. Children, in general, have a natural ability to hit the ball. It comes easily to them, and a child given a club that is the right size will have a great time hitting a golf ball for the first time.

I will always remember the first days of my golfing life. The joy never ended. Hit the ball as hard as you can and go get it! What a simple beginning. I will always love this game for its simplicity and ability to create memories for a lifetime.

Oh, the joy of zero expectations: hit the ball, hopefully forward and in play. Hit the ball often, and chase it till you drop. I was young enough not to know any better, and old enough to know you got better every day. I never kept score and always bragged about my last shot. My self-esteem rose to new heights daily, and the width of my smile increased with each successful swat, much to the delight of my parents.

My mom and dad always gave me words of encouragement, day-by-day helping me to learn more and enjoy the game more and never forcing me to keep score!

Years later, I would discover the joy of keeping score, then the wonders of breaking one hundred, then ninety, then eighty. I still haven't broken seventy. I have however shot seventy several times, and I still believe I will break it before my playing days are done.

The Joy of a Great Walk

How long has it been since the days of your youth, when you took a walk in the park with your mom or a stroll in the woods with your dad? Remember the joyous smile on your face that told your parents you loved them? If you could take that walk all over again, would you do it? Most of us would do it in an instant. The memories of the time spent with our parents in our youth are memories for a life-time.

I believe the game of golf is a game intended to be played walk-ing, the benefit of a good three and a half mile walk are well docu-mented today.

The art of walking the golf course was refreshed in my memory last year, when the United States Golf Association started a program to promote walking while playing golf. I challenge anyone who thinks they can play faster riding to keep track of the amount of time it takes to play with a cart and then play the same course walk-ing. Keep both times to verify my theory. Even if you have to use a trolley (pull cart), your exercise and enjoyment will increase.

Some years ago, at Walnut Creek Golf Course, I was ready to tee off with friends when the starter told the four of us walk-ons to take off before the first group got there. The first group was a riding foursome. And thinking four walkers would slow them down, to say they were mad is a great understatement. Now, I was the highest handicap at eight, and we could all strike the ball! Three hours and twenty minutes later, we were sitting in the clubhouse, when the group came in at the four-hour mark. One of them said, "Past the second fairway, we never saw anyone. What did you guys do, *run?*"

I assured them—and will assure you—we didn't run, nor did we ever stop. We all hit our ball when it was our turn and moved on at a good pace. If one of us was in trouble, the next closest person took their shot and then we continued.

Playing a golf course is a beautiful, joyous walk among the trees, animals, and streams of this great nation. Every hole is waiting for us to enjoy, and learn more about ourselves, while we play God's game to and for His glory.

I recommend everyone walking the golf course; it will do three basic things for you:

1. Slow you down so you can enjoy your surroundings in God's kingdom while you concentrate on your game.

2. Set a good pace at which you will play your best game.

3. Allow you to evaluate yourself and your performance on a shot-by-shot basis. This will enable you to improve your game as you go. A simple prayer from time to time will help you by eliminating those butterflies as you attempt to play your best game ever.

The Joy of a Game Played Well

When the game is properly played, the experience can only be described as joyous. That joy comes from

- knowing where the ball is going to go;
- knowing which club to use;
- knowing how to read the green;
- knowing how hard to hit a putt;
- knowing you can do all things through Christ, who strengthens all who follow him.

For those who don't care how they play, just play this wonderful game in the glory of God and enjoy your days in His presence.

However, taking several lessons from a PGA professional can improve your swing to the point that you will understand what you are doing, which will increase your joy of playing the game.

Take three to six lessons, so you can build on what you learn from one lesson to the next. This will enable you to create a lasting swing that you will enjoy for the rest of your life. After that, you should take a lesson every year to reinvigorate your game while getting ready for the season in the spring.

I take a lesson every spring, and then one a couple of weeks later. This allows me to get my game "back in shape." Then I am ready for the season. This is the best way to play the game well and enjoy it for years to come.

PEACE

To truly grasp the concept of peace on the golf course, one must first understand one's personal reaction to adversity, or RTA. RTA separates average golfers from the truly great golfers in the world. This is observed when you see that the professional golfer rarely shows any emotion when faced with making a truly horrific shot. What is your RTA when you hit one that is so badly shanked into the next fairway that it causes a double bogey? What is your RTA when you put your first tee shot out of bounds? Where does your RTA go when you place the ball in the pond on your favorite hole?

The inner peace that passes all understanding (Phil 4:7) is the true gift of the Holy Spirit that allows us to play great golf. That same peace that is in you through Jesus Christ at all times and in every way (2 Thes 3:16) will carry over to your golf game and allow you to improve on a regular basis.

The negative RTA, vibes, or nerves remind you of all your fears. These fears are the catalyst that unravels everyone's golf game—always.

For this reason, the need for peace of mind, peace within your heart, and in everything you do while on the course and in your everyday life is the single most important thing needed to play great golf all the time.

If you show me a man with true inner peace (demonstrated by a very positive RTA), I will show you a man with the potential to play the game well. He could play it well in all conditions and score well when he hasn't played in a while. This person is just going out to have some fun.

PATIENCE

Patience may well be the key element of the fruit that can enable anyone to play this game at a truly great level, and to score well for many years to come. I can honestly say that as a youth patience was missing from my vocabulary, let alone my golf game.

Like most youths, I could hit the ball a long way—with no idea where it would go. The reality was I didn't care. It was far more important to out-drive my dad than to keep my ball in play. My son is much the same way. With the positive response I give him for his long drives, I can see why I enjoyed the long bomb instead of the straight ball.

Hit it long down the fairway, out of bounds, extricate the club-head from below ground level, and reload. Take two strokes, take one more if I hit it in the water, and go on. Shoot eighty-five or ninety and go to the house happy that I outdrove my dad, even though he beat me convincingly. In a nutshell, my positive RTA was nonexistent.

Lack of patience to hit the ball down the middle is the main reason I could never beat my dad. I would rather go for broke than have him outdrive me. Patience at an early age would have made me a much better golfer. The patience to play within yourself, along with the understanding that one bad hole does not destroy a round, helps you play better golf. Better golf is the goal of everyone who loves to play the game.

Webster's Ninth New Collegiate Dictionary defines patience as "being steadfast despite opposition, difficulty, or adversity." Wow, is that ever a mouthful when you play this game. How many of us refuse to be patient, to try even harder after every adversity and difficult situation? My dad used to say, "One stroke at a time." Maintaining that attitude will help you play your best game. That's how a good game is played. Your most important stroke is the *next* one, right to the very end. This is the secret to truly great golf, and to a large degree, patience will get you through a good, if not great, round of golf.

I was once graced to hear a talk by golf coach Dave Williams of the University of Houston. The theme was "It's not how you start; it's how you finish" (Col 1:11, 12). That goes for life as well as golf, for it is written in the book of Romans, chapters 12: "Be joyful in hope, patient in affliction, faithful in prayer" and 13: "Share with God's people who are in need. Practice hospitality."

After all, we need to learn as we go to be patient in every situation. Patience should be incorporated into every aspect of course management, each and every time we play. We should learn early in the round the factors that will impact each day's game. These variables include the following:

- how the greens respond
- how the ball reacts to the grass
- how the wind works on that particular course
- how correct the yardage markers are
- how we feel during the game

All provide learning experiences. All are worthy of noting. And all will test how patient you can remain in the face of adversity and how you will respond to the few great strokes that you will hit. Be patent in all that you do, from the beginning, because a double bogey on hole number one is simply two over par. The patience to play great golf from that point forward could net you seventeen pars in a row, give or take a birdie or a bogey, which will give you a score of seventy-something—a very good round of golf.

If you are very patient in the beginning and take what the course will give you early, you will play better each day. Allow your patience to permeate your awareness of your pin placement. This will help you to hit the ball closer to the pin, even if you are off the green. Getting up and down in three gets you a bogey! You are still scoring well. It makes no sense to hit the ball to the center of the green, allowing it to roll to the back, when the pin is close to the front of the green. Most courses today have multicolored flags, or ball markers on the flagstick, that tell you their position on the green.

Being patient, playing one stroke at a time, one hole at a time, with the added patience of the Holy Spirit, will cause your day to go very well. Your scores will drop round by round, day by day, and help you grow ever closer to my Lord and Savior. And I pray he is yours, too!

KINDNESS

How in the world does kindness come into the game of golf—especially when you see the dog-eat-dog competition that continues on the course when two friends bring their verbal jabs and attitude to the course? Let me explain.

Kindness, for the golfer who plays at public courses, manifests itself in good deeds, such as picking up a person's clubs just off the green, giving your playing partner that three-foot putt when he hasn't made one all day. The always-popular returning a club that you find on the course to the pro shop at the end of your round is a great act of kindness.

In mental play (also called stroke play), that little gimmie putt will get you disqualified in tournament golf. In match play, it is legal; once the putt is given, it is good—even if your playing partner chooses to practice and misses the putt. Acts of kindness like these also improve the pace of play, making the game more enjoyable for all who love the game.

The little random acts of gentlemanly kindness are what separate golf from all other sports. They make the game enjoyable for people of all ages, no matter what their game is like or what their handicap may be (2 Pt 5:9).

GOODNESS

Be patient in all you do, and to those you play this wonderful game with, allowing the goodness of each round to come out in your daily life.

Be a cheerleader for those you play with, that they may play their best golf, while allowing you to enjoy God's game.

One of the greatest joys you can have is to beat someone on a great course while you root for them to play their best. Goodness comes into play with great sportsmanship. While on the course, you should understand that you represent yourself, your family, your home club (if you have one), and your Lord and Savior in all your actions on the course. Do everything with goodness in your heart. It makes everyone's day that much better.

FAITHFULNESS

Webster's Ninth New Collegiate Dictionary defines faithfulness as "the firm adherence to whatever one owes allegiance." And the first being we all owe faithfulness to is our God; Father, Son and the Holy Spirit. He is Our Lord and Savior. This is the only true allegiance in our lives.

As we play golf, we should be faithful to

- the traditions of the game;

- the rules of the game;

- the etiquette of the game;

- the spirit of the game.

These things are being left behind as the game becomes more popular. With the number of golf fans growing on a daily basis, the traditions, etiquette, and rules of the game are being questioned. Also, the less you know the game, its traditions, and its rules, the more difficult it is to understand the greatest game mankind has ever invented.

I challenge you to learn all four of these areas of the game while you come to enjoy the game more every day.

Greg Norman (and I am a great fan of his) once said, "In order to play great golf, you must be brutally honest with yourself." This is the main reason so many golfers play for years and never get any better. I will be the first to say if you enjoy shooting one hundred and have no desire to improve, great!

However, if you want to shoot seventy-something, please take Greg's advice and be faithful to the game. Read some books; take lessons, and practice, practice, practice. Remember the words of Vince Lombardi: "Practice doesn't make perfect; perfect practice makes perfect."

Go to church on Sunday morning; eat lunch with your family before you head for the first tee, and you will play better golf.

Take your children with you and learn to

- play better golf;
- be a better person;
- be an example to your children;
- be a blessing to those around you;
- be faithful to your Creator, Lord, and Savior.

In order for you to grow as a Christian, you must be brutally honest about where you are in your relationship with Jesus the Christ. Ask yourself the question, *am I growing closer to Him or am I moving farther away from Him?* I pray you choose to grow closer to Him day by day, until your personal relationship is one of being very close to Him

GENTLENESS

Gentleness is another key to playing great golf. Look at all the top golfers in the world. The adjective you will hear used to describe them all is "gentle."

"Gentle Ben" Crenshaw is the first player who comes to my mind, and his win at Augusta after the death of Harvey Penick is one of the greatest sports stories of all time. People continue to talk about Ben as being gentle in personality, a warrior in competition while always at peace with his surroundings.

My wife and I were sitting in Sunday school one day when the instructor asked a young lady (who happened to not be married) what she wanted in the man of her dreams.

Her statement, utterly simple, caught me by total surprise. Her response was, "I simply want a gentle man to love me and care for me." I was amazed, because her comment did not evoke thoughts in me of a mouse of a man, but rather a very strong man with hands of stone and a masculine nature to rival that of Hercules. The word "gentle" sets women's hearts ablaze, because most are searching for a man of gentle strength rather than a strong dictator who will prevent them from growing closer to the Lord. They hope for a man of God in pursuit of righteousness, godliness, faith, love, endurance, and gentleness (1 Tim 6:11; paraphrased). What woman wouldn't want a man of this nature?

You must have a gentle nature to play golf well, because the game is hard enough without taking it too seriously, which some men do.

This gentle nature allows one to make a mistake, understand it, and be accepting of the effects created by the mistake. This mentality must also be combined with the patience to understand that one stroke neither makes nor breaks a round.

SELF-CONTROL

Within the game, self-control is the wonderful element that fuses the fruit together like nectar in an orange.

Controlling one's emotions during a round of golf is the essential difference between the player who shoots a triple-digit score and the player who shoots a score in the low to mid-seventies. You probably have heard it said that the game is between the ears and wondered how that could be. Let me explain.

You diligently work on your game and have nothing to show for it after hours of practice. You take your practice game to the first tee and find yourself shooting another ninety-something. The difference lies in your ability to hone the best-kept secret of golf, the pre-shot routine. This is the ability to take dead aim, calm your emotions, and swing with an emotion-free tempo. This will put the ball on line, struck properly, with an inner peace that surpasses all understanding, as you play better golf stroke by stroke.

The following questions, when answered honestly, will bring your game to new heights:

1. Was your practice anywhere in the realm of perfect practice, which is defined as practice with meaningful purpose? What do you want to learn today as you practice? Have you learned that lesson today in an effort to make your practice perfect?

2. Were your practice shots executed the same way with each stroke? Was your routine the same for each shot? It is my opinion that the routine before each shot is as important as the shot itself.

3. Did you take "dead aim," as Harvey Penick says over and over again in his books? Take dead aim: line up a shot from behind the ball on a stick, a blade of grass, a stone—anything that will

give you a crosshair to put the ball on line, toward the pin, every time.

The numbers of people I have played with that have fairly good swings but who never break ninety is substantial. Their problem is simple: at the first bit of adversity, they begin to swear, throw clubs, complain about the speed of the greens, and give a zillion different excuses why their game isn't better that day.

Be brutally honest: if you're one of those people, then the main missing ingredient in your life and your golf game is self-control, no more, no less.

Ben Hogan was probably the most stoic person ever to play the PGA Tour, and as many people will tell you, if he made birdie or bogey you could never tell from his reaction. David Duval is much like that. Last year, when he shot his historic final round fifty-nine on a difficult course, an announcer asked him if he was going to warm up for a playoff. He replied in jest, "I think I have a few things I can work on!"

This is a very good lesson for every golfer who wants to play better golf. Keep your emotions in check until the last putt drops, and work on it in your daily life also. This is the one fruit of the spirit I see lacking in so many people. Golfers can't begin to understand why people question their Christianity when they show little self-control, and believe me, *they do notice a lack of self-control.*

All things included in expressing the fruit of the spirit enable you to play His game in a manner pleasing to our Lord and Savior: Jesus, the Christ.

TO COPE

To cope is the ability to deal with, and understand, your failures.

TO HOPE

Hope is the ability to understand with knowledge and faith that tomorrow will be better. To know the next second, minute, hour will be better. That eternity awaits. Tomorrow...

3

STRENGTH
OF THE GAME

I can do all things through Christ who strengthens me.

—(Phil 4:13)

In my personal experience, it takes an incredible amount of energy to be mentally tough enough to shoot a low number when you do not have your "A" game. There are days when you play like a hack and still shoot a low score because you are able to recover from the bad shots that could (or should) cause you to shoot a high score. Examples of this include the bad tee shot on one hole that seems not to hurt you but would be out of bounds on the next hole and cost you two strokes. This is the most misunderstood reality of golf: the "what if" syndrome. Let's look at the syndrome.

All of the above circumstances could be seen as luck, and yet it is important to understand the greatness of preparation before every shot. The ability to take "dead aim" shot after shot is the catalyst that allows you to play good golf even if your game is not at its best. Taking dead aim allows you to hit a ball less than perfectly with results good enough to get par on that hole. This mental toughness

18

has everything to do with your positive mental attitude, your ability to relax, and your ability to score. Let's look at some ways you can improve your mental toughness without engaging your nervous system.

Never, ever play the shot before you get to your ball. Consider the following scenario: you start to approach your ball, which is next to a 150-yard marker in the middle of the fairway, and you immediately start to pull out your seven-iron to execute your shot. You hit a near-perfect iron shot, only to find yourself fifteen yards short of the hole and off the green, with a very difficult pitch to the hole.

You look up at the flag position to see a blue flag indicating the pin is in the back third of a thirty-yard-long green. Further evaluation reveals the ground is not level and you were on an uphill slope, causing you to lose distance when you struck the ball. Analyzing this dilemma, you discover the correct club would have been more like a five-iron, to execute the shot in a way that would get the ball to the pin. Always, always, always use enough club to get the ball to the hole, and you will play better golf—you'll score better too. Remember to take more club on an up-slope and less club on a down-slope. Mental toughness is the state of mind that allows you to make a correct decision most of the time. You must also be able to equate every wrong decision with the loss of a stroke.

One of the primary failures of high-handicap golfers is getting the ball to the hole on their approach shot on a regular basis. This lack of mental toughness is primarily due to many improperly analyzed situations. The high-handicap golfer always believes his next stroke will be perfect. The low-handicap golfer understands that he will only hit four to six perfect shots in a round. The rest will be near-perfect. Hence, the high-handicap player always expects to hit a perfect shot; the low handicapper will always understand that his shot will be nearly, but seldom, perfect.

You will hear the high-handicap golfer say, "Gee, I hit that ball well." Seldom will you hear him say, "I hit that ball perfectly." Ben Hogan said, "If I hit six perfect shots a round, that is excellent for me." If Ben only hit six out of sixty-two to seventy-four shots perfectly, he hit 90 percent of his shots nearly perfectly.

How can anyone think they will hit a perfect shot more often than the great Ben Hogan? It just doesn't make a lot of sense. However, as stated in Philippians, you can do these things through Christ. The most important thing is to ask yourself the right questions before you take your stroke, and always take "dead aim."

This author challenges you, when you hit the course, to see things developing. Ask yourself to pray more about the things that matter to you: your wife, friends, and situations in life—anything to allow you to grow closer to Jesus Christ. Take your mind off of the next shot and what score you might shoot, until you get to your ball. Then analyze. Take dead aim, execute the shot to the best of your ability, and when finished simply say, "Thank you, Lord, for this beautiful day, and for allowing me to play this great game of yours. Amen."

4

THE WILL TO PLAY THE GAME

Hence, I remind you to rekindle the gift of God that is within you through the laying on of my hands; for God did not give us a spirit of timidity but a spirit of power, love and self control.

—(2 Tim 1:6–7)

In my son's room, there is a marble placard with this prayer:

> *God, grant me the serenity to accept the things I cannot change,*
> *The courage to change the things I can,*
> *And the wisdom to know the difference.*

The spirit of timidity that Paul speaks of is not about a personal attribute, but rather your relationship with the Father when you are told (spoken to) to act on His behalf. *Do not* be timid, but rather act decisively with love and self-control.

These are some of my favorite words in the Bible, because so often we hear the words of our Father and do nothing to act. Paul says, "Go for it; act NOW when the Lord says 'Go!'"

The ability and will to stay the course is the essence of the Christian life and requires complete dedication to the teachings of Jesus, the Christ.

Likewise, few of us act when given the blatant knowledge that our game is slipping. We do nothing to improve our game or ourselves, even as the game teaches us more and more about ourselves.

So many times we try to change the things we cannot change. We act as if pushing ourselves to hit the perfect shot will erase the truly horrible shot we just hit into the water or, worse yet, out of bounds. We refuse to accept our fate, but rather try the impossible shot to somehow correct the fate we have just been handed. The ability to accept our plight and the courage to do the right thing and play for the meaningful completion of the hole with the least amount of damage is, in fact, an answer to prayer. This allows us to complete that hole and start the next one on level ground, to start our string of pars or birdies all over again.

Every player should strive to do their very best through Jesus Christ, every time they go out. This is truly difficult, as it requires the will to perform at your very best each and every time you play. To play golf at this level is a very demanding mental requirement (toughness) that few of us can comprehend without the help of a close relationship with the father.

The pros simply call it "taking it deep," meaning once you get under par, staying there and going further under with each hole. The mental discipline that equates to staying in the zone takes incredible focus. The will to stay the course is the essence of great golf.

5

HOPE IN
THE GAME

Through him we have obtained access to this grace in which we stand, and we rejoice in our hope of sharing the glory of God. More than that, we rejoice in our sufferings, knowing that suffering produces endurance, and endurance produces character, and character produces hope, and hope does not disappoint us, because God's love has been poured into our hearts through the Holy Spirit which has been given to us.

—(Rom 5:2–5)

Here's another question that explains why golf is such a tough game to master and play well: Rejoice in our suffering? For many who play golf, that is very difficult to do!

You hit the best tee shot of your life, only to watch it roll into a pond standing two hundred and fifty yards from the tee, and you start complaining about what a bad break! And yet you never think about the near-perfect shot you just hit. But in reality, it's a simple problem to fix.

You drop a ball; incurring a one-stroke penalty, hit a six- or seven-iron to the green and two-putt for bogey. All this on a hole on which you would have gladly taken a bogey to start with if you hadn't hit the ball in the water off the tee. If you get lucky and make a putt, par is your score.

To score well, you should *never* look back on your last shot. You can do nothing about it except better execute your next shot or understand that the outcome of your next shot may be more to your liking. In everyday life, and especially in golf, you must take the good with the bad (no matter how distasteful) and respond with the character that comes from a personal relationship with Jesus Christ. Each round of golf gives us the hope for a better tomorrow, or at least a better next shot.

As long as we are talking about improvement, it should be noted that the game is indeed difficult, and so I say that

- any golf shot that advances forward is indeed a good shot;

- any shot advanced forward and in the correct direction toward the pin is a great shot;

- any shot forward with the correct distance and the right direction is truly an excellent shot.

No matter who makes that excellent shot, it is worthy of applause! It will lighten your day and will let the person know that he or she did an excellent job! Don't you wish sometimes that people at work would applaud you for a great job, *just once*?

Hope and *character*—developing these two attributes will allow you to play better golf.

6

THIS IS YOUR LIFE

Love is:
Patient and kind
Not jealous or boastful
Not arrogant or rude
Not irritable or resentful
Love does not:
Insist on its own way
Rejoice at wrong

Love:
Rejoices in the right
Bears all things
Hopes all things
Endures all things

—(1 Cor 13:4–7, paraphrased)

Faith, hope, love, these three:
But the greatest of these is love.

—(1 Cor 13:13)

Tom Watson once said, "Golf is the game of life in eighteen holes." So, why do we play this wonderful game? This is a complex question in many a golfer's mind. Many players love the game, and many more claim to hate it, but no one would play a game they hated for very long without serious mental damage.

For more than a hundred years, wives have wondered why their husband's play a game they cannot win. A spouse can be a golfer's biggest fan and yet still wonder why they play a game they cannot win. Your spouse is your biggest fan and asks the most questions about why you play a game you cannot win. Golfers play because they **love** the game! The thrill of hitting that one great shot, or the victory of that one pure shot amid all the lousy ones we see each and every time we play, is the one joyous occasion that keeps us playing this great game.

The difference between our game and that of the touring pro is simple: their lousy shots are far better than our very best ones, and their very best ones are, at the very least, miraculous!

We love the game as we love our spouse, our children, our parents; our friends—anyone near and dear to our hearts hold a similar place in our heart.

The game is:

- maddening at times;
- joyous at times;
- humbling at times;
- terrific all the time;
- the ultimate love affair with a game you can never win!

Let's look at the words of Paul in Corinthians as we ponder or play the game we all love.

Love *is patient and kind.* In golf, the more patience we show during our round, the better chance we have to play great golf. Lack of patience will force us to try too hard, to try to hit the perfect shot. Instead, we should take our medicine at the time and work to post the lowest score possible for that hole. The harder we try, the worse we play; patience is the key to great scores. One bad hole does not make a round. Whether the bad hole is first or last does not make a difference. Seventeen more pars and you still have a good round; hence, patience is the key to great scoring. Patience is the key to better play, because we understand how *love* works in our life and how we must *love* the game to truly play it well.

Love *is not jealous or boastful.* Wow! What a statement, as we all have, from time to time, boasted of that terrific shot, only to hit that career worst shot with the next stroke like never before. In 1986, I hit my one and only hole in one (I'm not boasting, just relating to the story), only to stand on the next tee with so much happiness that I hit the next two balls in the water, didn't even care, and pulled a snowman (posted an eight on the scorecard) out of my hat, as I was the happiest man on the course! So, as you think about boasting, just remember, your next snowman is just around the corner and you may or may not be happy to see him. With every good golfer has gone hundreds of hours of training and practice to get to a level of play he or she can be proud of—and that person may or may not have all the blessings you have.

Love *is not arrogant or rude.* Golf is *thee* gentleman's game. You need look no further than your television set to see that the truly great players of the world are gentlemen, in every sense of the word. From what most of us know, the great players tend to be gentlemen both on and off the course, and very few people say anything unkind about them—ever!

Love *is not irritable or resentful.* Neither is the true golfer when his partner beats him like a rented mule and everyone makes fun of him for the bad round he shot that day. It is important to note that great players understand ***they play the course***, not their playing partner that day. Some days a player beats the course and some days the course gets the best of the player. Golf is a gentleman's game, and if your playing companions are gentlemen, then you don't need to worry about them making fun of your round.

Play the game as a gentleman or lady and as if you are in the presence of your Lord and Savior, because you are!

In our daily life, we so seldom understand—or see—the difference we make when we realize the only one we need to please is the Lord, who made us!

The game of golf is much like a great love affair, and the course is the obstacles we face in our daily walk, with all its problems, joys, hazards, hopes, and dreams. The faith we have in our golf swing after hours and hours of practice, both on the range and on the practice green gives us the ability to play at the highest level. Golf requires you to love the game in order to play it well. It requires you to practice, be patient, be kind, be full of faith, hope, and charity, to play it well with a smile on your face and love in your heart.

I challenge everyone who reads this book to take a good look at these verses in the Bible and start living your life with more love than you ever thought possible. Understanding the words, and living by them, will make you a much better and happier person with the joy of the Holy Spirit present in your life.

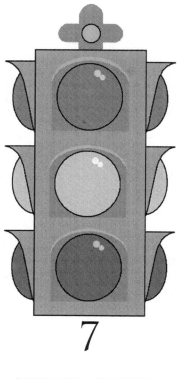

7

THE GIFT

For God so loved the world that he gave his one and only Son that whoever believes in him shall not perish but have eternal life.

—(John 3:16)

Relax. It's not a misprint; this is the same way I started the book. The reason for this is because life and eternity is all about the gift. We love and cherish the game we play, and no game can hold a candle to the joy our families bring us on a daily basis.

Daily we confront all the problems, cares, trials, tribulations, joys, loves, and hopes that come our way. So daily we must build our relationships to gain the endurance needed to finish the good fight. In the end, our hope is to be with our Lord and Savior when our last day comes. On the other side, we will meet Jesus face to face in the hope we can hear him say, "Well done, good and faithful servant."

Some people would allow you to believe that works make a difference in your life. If you do all the good works you are capable of, you may be lucky enough to inherit eternal life. The amount of work it would take to reach the goal of eternal life through works is impossible to estimate.

The thought process to justify works as a means of salvation would require the balance sheet of a lifetime. Only God could possibly keep track of that good and bad balance sheet. The Bible tells us that God gave his Son so that we can have eternal life. This is as simple as it gets, "for it is not by works we are saved, but by grace" (Eph. 2:8–9).

This reality comes equipped with the added statement from Ephesians, "lest anyone should boast." You see, to have a full and meaningful relationship with God comes so very easily; you simply admit to being a sinner (for it is written in Romans 3:23: "for all have sinned and fall short of the glory of God"). Accept Jesus as your Lord and Savior. Invite Jesus, the Christ, to live in your heart. These actions, coupled with a change in your life to live for Him, read His text (the Bible), grow closer to him, and gain a close personal relationship with the God of the universe and give you the knowledge that you will inherit eternal life. As a believer, in time, you will develop all of the attributes within the fruit of the Spirit.

I would recommend you ask Him into your life and each day ask Him to stay close (pray daily, unceasingly even), and He will reveal his will for your life, each and every day. Grow closer to Him with each passing day, and someday, someone will walk up to you and say, "You have really changed." You can then say with pride, "Yes, by the grace of God I have changed, and I am a much better person for it." You see, it takes all the attributes within the fruit of the Spirit to play great golf, and it takes all the fruit of the Spirit to truly show the light of Christ through your eyes for the entire world to see.

I pray you know my Lord and grow ever closer to Him. Play great golf! Live the life God intended you to have and may God bless you.

As you begin your new life with Christ I invite you to look into the Gospels with me as it relates to your relationship with the Father.

Now, with the help of the Holy Spirit, I will give you a completely different view, that of a child as it relates to your heavenly Father. This insight will give you a new light into the newness of life that everyone looks for to complete his or her life and make it fulfilling in every way.

Proverbs can give us a base to better play the game that God has given to his children to enjoy and help them better understand themselves, their relationships, and their feelings.

8

PROVERBS FOR GOLF AND LIFE (THE WISDOM OF GOD)

Wisdom calls aloud in the street, she raises her voice in the public squares;
at the head of the noisy streets she cries out, in the gateway of the city she makes her speech:
"If you had responded to my rebuke, I would have poured out my heart to you and made my thoughts known to you."

—(Prb 1:20, 21, 23)

Praying for wisdom allows us, especially as parents, to invoke the work of the Holy Spirit, allowing our children to learn from our mistakes. His wisdom, imparted to them, can make their lives better, should they choose to learn.

How many of us, deaf to the wisdom of our God, go through life trying to do it ourselves? God the Father is waiting to hear our cry, and He guarantees a response. James 1:5 says we simply need to ask for His wisdom.

How many of us ask? How many of us know to ask?

Ask the Father for wisdom, and life can suddenly become easier. We simply need to listen and act upon his gift.

James 1:5 tells us, "If any of you lacks wisdom, he should ask God, who gives generously to all without finding fault, and it will be given to him."

Golf, though a game, becomes easier, too, when we listen and act with wisdom, concentration, and relaxation. Wisdom in golf is necessary to be able to make the right decision most of the time. Having wisdom to ask yourself the right questions when approaching a shot will take many strokes off your game by eliminating the shot that costs you several strokes on one hole.

The ability to eliminate the double bogey is the key to great scoring. Many times at the end of a round, shooting eighty or eighty-one, the people in my foursome tell me I played terrible and still shot a good score. The secret is simple: if you can avoid the large numbers during a round of golf, a good score becomes easy.

> *"My son, if you accept my words and store up my commands within you, Turning your ear to wisdom and applying your heart to understanding, and if you call out for insight and cry aloud for understanding, and if you look for silver and search for hidden treasure, then you will understand the fear of the Lord and find the knowledge of God."*

—(Prb 2:1–5)

"Accept my words and store up my commands within you." HOW HARD IS THAT? Yet we continue to go through life with the "I can do it myself" syndrome. If only we listened and acted without timidity to do his will. We often pray, listen, get an answer, and "do what we want to do." How sad it is when we do not listen. How many times have you made that statement in regard to your children? How many times has God the Father made that statement about you?

Golf is much the same way. We go through the questions of what to do on any given shot, and then we attempt to make the impossible shot we know is truly impossible. This results in a snowman or double-digit score that knocks us out of our right to reach our personal lowest score. My first prayer and wish is that you will listen to the knowledge of the players who came before you. Play within your talents and shoot that new lowest score. Make it the standard, and go on, in the future, to a new low number you have longed to attain.

The writing of this book has been much like the above statements. The Holy Spirit has prodded me to finish it, and all the other things in my life have kept its completion from occurring in a timely manner.

Its completion has finally occurred since I now understand the need to listen and obey. Beth Moore, at a James Robinson (the head of Life Outreach International) taping, made it clear to me that I need to finish the book for the sake of my Lord and Savior Jesus the Christ to further the kingdom of the Father. The ability to listen to the will of the Holy Spirit and to pray like we are children to do His will, every day will help us in our daily walk with Him. We must listen and obey in order to do the will of the Father.

> *"'My son, do not forget my teaching, but keep my commands in your heart, for they will prolong your life many years and bring you prosperity.'"*
>
> —(Prb 3:1, 2)

> *"Blessed is the man who finds wisdom, the man who gains understanding, for she is more profitable than silver and yields*

better returns than gold, She (wisdom) is more precious than
rubies; nothing you desire can compare with her."

—(Prb 3:13–15)

The need to hear and obey our heavenly Father is as common a notion as a child needing to obey his earthly father. How many of us, however, fail to take the time to pray and listen for the answers from our heavenly father? Take the time during your golf game to pray and listen to the quiet tones of nature and hear your Father in heaven speaking to you.

Nothing in golf will lower your score faster than wisdom and patience within the knowledge of your personal game. Most golfers can lower their score with the knowledge of what wisdom can accomplish during any one round of golf.

This can be done by answering one simple question: *At what yardage, in the fairway, am I comfortable getting down from in three strokes or less?*

Answering this question allows you to position the ball at a given yardage to do no worse than score a bogey. For most of us, the ability to get out of trouble with nothing worse than a bogey will be the best thing for our golf game since we took up the game and started counting strokes correctly. For the experienced player (watch the pros), the question is, *what can I do to get inside the one-hundred-yard marker?* The pros and the good golfers know it will be only two or three strokes at the most to put the ball in the hole from that spot.

This simple suggestion, if taken to heart, and used with wisdom, will lower your score in a dramatic way. For those players who can't break one hundred, this process will break that number, then ninety, and possibly eighty. The reality of wisdom used in golf does not come easy. Nothing comes easy in golf without practice.

The player who wants to break ninety or eighty consistently without practice is a fool! Harsh words, but nonetheless true.

"Practice does not make perfect. Perfect practice makes perfect." (Vince Lombardi)

> *"Do not forsake wisdom, and she will protect you; love her, and she will watch over you. Wisdom is supreme; therefore get wisdom. Though it cost all you have, get understanding. Esteem her, and she will exalt you; embrace her, and she will honor you."*
>
> —(Prb 4:6–8)

Wisdom, the ultimate gift, by the grace of God! Do *you* ever ask for the gift? "If any of you lacks wisdom, he should ask God, who gives generously to all without finding fault, and it will be given to him." (James 1:5)

The power to introduce understanding in difficult situations, with the reality that the Lord is with you in every situation, will result in the understanding that you are a child of God!

When you play golf, it is incredibly important to gain wisdom in all aspects of your game. The attempt at the impossible shot is *not* the best way to help your score. Better yet, the play made with wisdom will result in the removal of the dreaded "6, 8, X," vulture (two times par) from your scorecard. The ability to bring more wisdom into your game will improve your scoring more than you are willing to admit. You may not play any better, but you will score better.

How often have you said, "This is going to be my best round ever," only to start your round with one bad shot, followed by the random attempt at the "perfect recovery shot"? That little misgiving sets an "X" on the card in lead, and your "best game ever" is gone before you finish the third hole. Let's look at some good advice.

When in trouble off the tee, pray for wisdom, and find a way to get your ball to the one-hundred-yard marker, or simply in the fairway at a reasonable distance. Now ask yourself, *How often can I get down in three strokes from a hundred yards?* When your game supports getting up and down in three strokes more often than not, you will start to score better with wisdom and some common sense.

Even if you simply get the ball to the fairway and you are two hundred yards out, you should be able to get it in the cup with four strokes. Six is two strokes better than eight and four strokes better than ten. Isn't golf—and life—great?

Please take the time to study Proverbs. With only thirty-one chapters, it is easy to read one chapter every two or three days. Within two months, you will gain knowledge of the Old Testament while reading of the wisdom of Solomon.

Proverbs can help all aspects of our life and give us insight into our relationships with others that transcends understanding. The gift is from God, simply for the reading.

> *"He who oppresses the poor shows contempt for their Maker,*
> *but whoever is kind to the needy honors God."*

> —(Prb 14:31)

This verse is highlighted in my Bible with the knowledge that each of us should always be kind to the poor and needy. In the sight of the Lord, we are all worms when compared with the glory of the Lord. The way we look at the world gives us insight into how we view the world and how committed we are to the great commission.

How in the world can this verse be related to golf? Let me count the ways! When golf becomes more than a game, the "win at all costs" syndrome engulfs our selfishness in our own purpose.

The best way to view this verse is by treating your partner like the oppressed poor. When the time comes to give him that three-foot putt, you give it to him or her with an open heart and expecting nothing in return. Then you should come away with the understanding that he is not obligated to give you the three-foot putt you are waiting to hit.

If you ask me for that putt, I will gladly give it to you—if only to see the stunned look on your face!

The joy in playing golf comes with the understanding that all people are equal. There are no poor players on the course. Some players know more about the game and some players know less, but all are different. The great player is a student of the game, while the poor player is learning the game for the sake of the game, and will in time learn to love it. The learning process is a journey with the course as the opponent, understanding that it is a game that cannot be won, simply enjoyed. It is God's game to be enjoyed.

So, enjoy it and understand that the person you are playing with is your friend, even if it is for only four hours! The fact remains; we are all friends in the sight of the Lord. We should all be brothers in Christ in everything we do; whether it is work or play, church family or real family, we all are given the same directive.

"Love the Lord your God with all your heart" and "love your neighbor as yourself." (Mat 22:37, 39)

The fact remains, the difference between rich and poor can be as short as a couple of days. If you don't understand this statement, ask anyone who has lived through the Depression, or the oil collapse of the mid-eighties in Houston, Texas, when one in three people were unemployed due to the sudden decline in the price of crude oil that made it uneconomical to produce. That is the true test of God's goodness and grace. Our actions, when a friend is in need, are the true test of our Christian witness.

"A gentle answer turns away wrath, but a harsh word stirs up anger.

The tongue of the wise commends knowledge, but the mouth of the fool gushes folly.

The eyes of the Lord are everywhere, keeping watch on the wicked and the good."

—(Prb 15:1–3)

The PGA is a unique fellowship of men given the incredible task of playing a gentleman's game and being required to behave like one. Add to this the infinite number of stupid questions that the attention-seeking members of the media can ask, and you then have one huge dichotomy that is difficult to believe.

From Tom Lehman to the late Payne Stewart, so many members of the PGA answer these questions with the poise and patience of Jobe. These "saints of the fairways," with few exceptions, answer each question with candor. Most of them present gentle words that can be as mellow as music. And sometimes these words should be delivered with the bluntness of a spear or a sharp javelin to the mid-section. This incredible situation continues fifty-two weeks a year with no let-up except when the player retires to the locker room for some relief from the not-so-well-meaning, or understanding, press corps members.

Some of these questions include gems like, "How did it feel to miss that four-foot putt for the Masters title?" Most of us would respond, "You idiot, it felt like gobbledygook."

Yet PGA members consistently come forth with the wisdom of Solomon to give the reporter a much better level of answer than is deserved. Each playing member of the PGA, whether they admit it or not, acknowledges the responsibility they have to the game by always putting their best foot forward.

To the Christian living in the real world, the probability of a "best foot forward" is not as consistent as it is for the Tour player. How often do we forget to pray for wisdom and simply jack our jaw for the sake of the last word?

All people should take note of the character of the PGA Tour players. These players play the game they choose as their career under the pressure of having to perform at their peak every day, knowing if they do not perform well, they will not get a paycheck.

The ability to pray and gain wisdom is always there! We simply need to ask and listen. The reality of witnessing for the Lord is part of the great commission we all have been given. "Go forth and make disciples of all nations" is not a request; it is a directive from Jesus the Christ.

> *"Gray hair is a crown of splendor; it is attained by a righteous life. Better a patient man than a warrior, a man who controls his temper than one who takes a city."*
>
> —(Prb 16:31–32)

The quality that most PGA professionals, and almost all low-handicap golfers, have in common is the ability to control their tempers during adverse circumstances. A true look at such a player shows the calm of a sunny day with the placid look of a Sunday stroll. All these players understand one common truth: patience is the key to great golf!

The ability to control your temper, attacking when appropriate and retreating when necessary, is the essence of golf played at its very best. The beauty of a great drive is a true joy. The decision to go long over the trap to avoid a "sucker pin" is one sign of good judgment. The ability to two-putt for a good par with a tap-in one-putt is a sign of common sense. The knowledge to not attack that pin can be interpreted as a sign of wisdom.

The best advice I can give the average golfer is shoot for the center of the green. This will allow you to gain confidence knowing:

- you are always putting

- if you three-putt, you still have bogey. Eighteen bogeys gets you ninety. All average golfers will take ninety or the mid-eighties and be very happy with their results.

So, stay calm, play intelligently, stay focused, and your game will improve dramatically. The biggest statement I can make is, an *average game and a great mind beats most players every day.*

> *"He who mocks the poor shows contempt for their Maker; whoever gloats over disaster will not go unpunished."*
>
> —(Prb 17:5)

This is the rule of the undisciplined golfer! The Lord was obviously speaking of the poor people in the world. It can also be applied to the golf world.

A golfer who delights in the ill-fated shots of others is destined to live the reality of the disasters to come. When your concentration gets broken and your errant shot is the result of recklessness, you get what you deserve. The player who plays his own game during the round will win out over adversity. The player who gives his opponent more than he deserves will find the benefits of a putt that drops, or an errant shot that ends perfectly with the "dues paying bounce," or the carom that ultimately saves strokes.

> *"Stop listening to instruction, my son, and you will stray from the words of knowledge."*
>
> —(Prb 19:27)

Understanding the fact that "you can't see yourself swing" is the awakening that leads a good player to become a great player. It can only let you admit the need for every golfer to seek instruction for their golf swing. I am shocked as I see golf pros who teach golf the way they play themselves and NOT teach the best swing for their student's stature and abilities. True PGA professionals should ask a group of questions before your lesson. Among these can be simple questions like the following:

- what do you hope to gain from this lesson?
- are you right-handed? How do you play golf, right-handed or left-handed?
- are you willing to work on your game diligently to improve to the next level?

If you were advising an engaged couple that needed counseling before marriage, I would hope you would suggest they go to their minister. Or at the very least a couple with thirty to fifty years of marriage experience to give them insight into their new relationship.

Your golf swing is the same. If you were a high-handicap golfer, would you take a lesson from your high-handicap friend, or a golf pro, or a three-handicapper? (By the way, a three-handicap golfer should know never to give a lesson to anyone who is a good friend or a relative. He would advise you to go to a golf pro, because the low-handicap golfer knows the hard work it takes to get to a low handicap. Are you willing to spend the time and effort to get there?

> *"Train a child in the way he should go, and when he is old he will not turn from it."*

*"Do not make friends with a hot-tempered man, do not asso-
ciate with one easily angered, or you may learn his ways and
get yourself ensnared."*

—(Prb 22:6, 24–25)

Many people know the words of this proverb from the Christian
comedian Mark Lowry, who discusses his father's study of the Bible
and his realization that correction is good for children.

This proverb goes to the golf course also, as most great golfers
began playing the game at a very young age. With proper teaching,
they have become the best players of the game. Likewise, the per-
sonalities of these players are mostly docile. Anger never enters into
their demeanor on the golf course. They seldom interact with anyone with a hot temper or build a rapport with people with that type
of personality and demeanor. They surround themselves with
proper, consistent, godly behavior.

I pray that each of you applies your heart to instruction and your
ears to the words of knowledge. Read your Bible; understand the
Lord's love for you and your family. Understand also that in order
to truly play great golf, instruction is a requirement, and the knowledge you gain will add to your enjoyment of the game. Each time
you gain knowledge, you will make yourself a better golfer and a
better person.

Showing or living the fruit of the Spirit is the sign of a true
Christian and the sign of a good golfer. The good golfer may not be
a Christian, but he will exemplify the attributes a Christian should
show to the world.

To be a great father and a good Christian, the attributes of Christ
should be in your heart. Christ should live in your heart, with the
intercession of the Holy Spirit, as you develop as a follower of Jesus,
the Christ.

Allow God's loving word to enter your life, that you can be a Christ-like person and a great father with a good golf game to show the world you have your priorities straight.

Put God first, then family, and live life to the fullest. Never put golf first or second, or third, but enjoy the game so that you can enjoy life and your family. Enjoy your family and your personal relationship with the God of the universe.

> *"Do not exalt yourself in the king's presence, and do not claim*
> *a place among great men;*
> *It is better for him to say to you, 'Come up here,' than for him*
> *to humiliate you before a nobleman."*

—(Prb 25:6, 7)

How many of us are willing to tell the world our golf game is any good? The reality is, for most of us, our game isn't very good. That one shot in a million we once hit is in dire need of a current instant replay.

The Lord tells us not to "blow our own horn" but rather tell the world the truth about ourselves. In a golf video Greg Norman said it best: "To play great golf you must be brutally honest with yourself." So, too, each of us must be brutally honest with ourselves in regard to our relationship with our Lord and Savior. Do you have a vibrant and living relationship with the Lord, or are you living the story of a one-way relationship? The Lord is there for you. Are you there for the Lord when He speaks to you of His will? Are you listening when He whispers and do you listen to his calling? The Lord is always there for you, ready to listen, should you decide to pray and come into fellowship with Him.

It is far better for Him to ask you to come to His table and fellowship with Him than for Him to say, "I know him not." The world is full of Sunday-morning Christians who make the show and do little, or nothing, for the kingdom.

So, my fellow golfers, get up and stand up for the Lord. Tell the world you love Him and have a living relationship with the God of the universe. This is the greatest witness you can make, to tell people that they, too, can have the same personal relationship you have. When they choose to invite Him into their hearts and live with Him, for Him, you will become a child of the living God.

> *"As iron sharpens iron, so one man sharpens another.*
> *As water reflects a face, so a man's heart reflects the man."*
>
> —(Prb 27:17, 19)

Promise Keepers is a Christ-centered organization dedicated to introducing men to Jesus Christ as their Savior and Lord and helping them to grow as Christians. One of the recommendations Promise Keepers makes for men is to develop a small integrity group of members who hold each other responsible for their actions and keep each other on the right path. I had no idea this verse, in Proverbs, was there, let alone so direct in the mission to bringing men together and holding each other accountable!

The game of golf is a walk in the park; each game is a training class in living life. The walk is a walk within a walk: a private walk while you play the course, and a social walk to be in the fellowship of each other. This dichotomy of "aloneness" and togetherness rests within the mind of the player. You walk within the natural environment of the course, alone, while the time spent in camaraderie of fellowship brings players closer together.

In the reality of a man's heart is the mirror of his character. Understanding your emotions will help you get closer to your heart. The reality is that God loves you, and the closer you grow to Him the closer your personal relationship will be to His glory! This produces a real and ultimately intimate relationship with the God of the universe.

YES, you can have a personal relationship with the God of the universe. It is a wonderful gift for you to receive. You need only to accept the gift given to you by the shed blood of Jesus, the Christ!

> *"A greedy man stirs up dissension,*
> *But he who trusts in the Lord will prosper.*
> *He who trusts in himself is a fool,*
> *But he who walks in wisdom is kept safe."*
>
> —(Prb 28:25, 26)

How many of us chase the elusive golden carrot only to discover the reality that the carrot has no life? The chase is part of the worldly game. What we finally discover is that the loss of family time leads to a very miserable person! This reality of life brings home the message that God and family are our most important possessions. Only after we discover the lies of the world do we understand that it is the chase for the carrot that separates us from the very people we love and care about.

The words of Proverbs tell us wisdom is the only way to avoid the trials of the world! It's amazing that people wish to have a family and then chase the "brass ring" on the carousel, only to discover the loss of everything when their partner gets tired of "doing it all themselves." The ability to help and spend time with your children is the most important gift you can give to your children.

Allow me a moment to give you some fatherly advice. My daughter will be married soon. I have one of the best relationships a dad could ever have with his daughter. I believe this is primarily due to the walks we took when she was little, followed by the talks we had (I mostly listened) while my "little girl" told me all the ills of the world as a teenager. Then she let me explain to her that life just isn't fair. The one thing a father can give to his children is his time! Time, the only priceless thing we have to give! You can't get it back once you give it; you can't find the secret to allow you to get more of it in the future.

The reality we must live as adults is the fact that kids want our time more than anything! It is my opinion that children whose parents spend time with them are more well rounded, better informed, and much closer to their parents. Parents have a much better ability to communicate with them in those adolescent years and help them grow closer to God.

PAY ATTENTION, MEN!

Look no further than your own time capsule to uncover the secret of a wonderful, loving, and giving relationship with your family. The relationship is a direct result of the time you are willing to give the people who mean the most to you!

Take time to call your parents, your siblings, and friends, so that in the future you don't lose those relationships that all of us need in "old age."

What does all this have to do with golf? Simple: the game can take time away from your family instead of bringing it closer together. When you play the game and your kids are old enough to go with you, take them with you and enjoy your time together.

Live life, love your family, and enjoy ALL your time together, *always!*

> *"Every word of God is flawless; he is a shield to those who take refuge in him.*
> *Do not add to his words, or he will rebuke you and prove you a liar."*

—(Prb 30:5, 6)

Ben Hogan helped write (with the help of Sports Illustrated) *Five Lessons: The Modern Fundamentals of Golf* It is the Bible of the golf swing; I recommend it to everyone who plays the game.

Likewise, the Bible is the Lord's book and needs no added inventory to the words we read. In Revelation, we read that not a word is to be added to His word. Likewise, in the Old Testament, we read the same words warning us to be diligent and correct in our studies of His Bible. We should understand and direct our lives to grow ever closer to Him and ever more knowledgeable of His will in our lives. The primary goal in our lives, living with Christ in our heart, is to grow ever closer to Him! To do His will, in His time, with His wisdom, under His peace that passes all understanding.

His book, the Bible, is all you really need to read!

9

JESUS SENDS OUT THE SEVENTY-TWO

"After this the Lord appointed seventy-two others and sent them two by two ahead of him to every town and place where he was about to go.

He told them, 'the harvest is plentiful, but the workers are few. Ask the Lord of the harvest, therefore, to send out workers into His harvest field.

Go! I am sending you out like lambs among wolves.'"

"The seventy-two returned with joy and said, 'Lord, even the demons submit to us in your name.'"

—(Luke 10:1–3, 17)

Jesus sent forth seventy-two, two by two to every village and town. Simply put, Jesus sent out one eighteen-hole golf course full of foursomes, to change the world. They did just that! Even demons submit to His name. The reality of thirty-six twosomes changing the world is unbelievable to me, yet the Lord knows that one person, committed to excellence, empowered by the Holy Spirit, can change the world.

If one can change the world, seventy-two can easily change the world. Do you allow yourself to be empowered by the Holy Spirit? Do you pray daily for all the people you know who need prayer? Do you pray for those who ask you for prayer? Do you take the following opportunities to live by the example of Jesus? Do you

- comfort those who need comfort?
- bring a smile to those who need one?
- visit those who are hospitalized?
- hug the unhuggable?
- make a difference to those who need faith?
- witness to those who need a savior?
- be a blessing to those who need a blessing?

Believe in your savior and make a difference in the world.

Golf is not the greatest game because God gave it to us. It is the greatest game because it allows us to witness to an unsaved world. It allows us to witness to one person at a time, two by two, all the way to the throne of God.

10

THE GREAT COMMISSION

Then Jesus came to them and said, "All authority in heaven and on earth has been given to Me. Therefore go and make disciples of all nations, baptizing them in the name of the Father and the Son and the Holy Spirit, and teaching them to obey everything I have commanded you. And surely I am with you always, to the very end of the age."

—(Mt: 28:18–20)

The great commission is the last word in the Gospel of Matthew. It is the last words of Jesus, the Christ, as He stood on earth. These words in today's world are the most important directive the Lord gave to His followers.

As we become Christians, we become aware of the presence of the Holy Spirit, only to be turned away from society, or cast out, because of the reaction people have to our sharing of the gospel of Jesus, the Christ. People will call us right-wing, radical, Holy Rollers, and out of touch with the modern world.

Wouldn't it be wonderful if the followers of Christ had the same fervor about Christianity that golfers have about golf? What a sad statement to make about the followers of Jesus, or at least the majority of those I have met, or come in contact with on a regular basis.

The irony of this statement is that there is no better way to have four hours of uninterrupted peace enabling one to witness to a friend about the goodness of Jesus in their life. This capability can bring the gospel to millions with few problems, as a follower witnesses through deeds and actions on the course and relates simply to their friends by the simple admission that one is a follower of Christ.

The opening chapters of this book allow you to see the gospel in the playing of this great game. Now it is up to you to live the gospel, as you play the game you love on a regular basis. Actions always speak louder than words, and golf is no exception. Go, therefore, and acknowledge your Savior as the one true God and that your Savior who lives in your heart has changed your life.

What a better way to discuss the gospel with your friend as you walk the course, enjoying nature and expounding on the greatness of the Lord's creation? The universe and all the galaxies beyond the heavens are all a creation of the great I AM. This knowledge, casually stated in a round of golf, could go unnoticed in the big picture. However, these statements can open the minds of your counterparts to the possibility of their acceptance of Jesus as their personal Savior. The nurturing of the gospel comes in many ways. It is not our duty to hammer the gospel home. Our duty is to spread the news that Jesus Christ is Lord of all. The Holy Spirit will allow them to grow into fully developing followers of Christ.

At the dawn of Christianity, there were twelve. Only eleven were left at the time of the great commission:

- Simon

- His brother Andrew

- James, son of Zebedee

- His brother John

- Phillip

- Bartholomew

- Thomas

- Mathew, the tax collector

- James, son of Alpheus

- Thaddeus

- Simon, the zealot

- And, later, Paul, the apostle

These are the first twelve. Is your name on the list of those dedicated to the great commission? It is time for all of us to rekindle the power within us through Christ Jesus. Let us begin.

AMEN

This is the end of this most heartfelt effort at a literary piece of work. As an engineer, it was a difficult work, at best. The thing I most hope that you glean from this book is an understanding of what golf, as a game, can teach you about yourself.

Your growth as a person can be a wonderful journey as you read your Bible, become aware of the Holy Spirit in your life, and grow ever closer to our Lord and Savior Jesus Christ.

Reference books to help your game:

1. The Bible, your choice of version

2. The New Testament with Proverbs

3. *Ben Hogan's Five Lessons: The Modern Fundamentals of Golf*

4. Harvey Penick's *Little Red Book.*

5. The graduate level text of the golf swing is *The Fundamentals of Hogan*, by David Leadbetter

> *"Golf is deceptively simple and endlessly complicated. A child can play it well, and a grown man can never master it. Any single round of it is full of unexpected triumphs and seemingly perfect shots that end in disaster. It is almost a science, yet it is a puzzle without an answer. It is gratifying and tantalizing, precise and unpredictable. It requires complete concentration and total relaxation. It satisfies the soul and frustrates the intellect. It is at the same time rewarding and maddening, and it is the greatest game mankind has ever invented."*
>
> **—Arnold Palmer**

A special thanks goes out to Rosanne Frazee for her help in editing this manuscript.

A portion of the proceeds from this book goes to Promise Keepers and the USGA.
Tony Small can be reached for book signings and/or speaking engagements at t44tx@yahoo.com. The author will respond to your request quickly.

INDEX

Note: References to Proverbs are in italics in order to differentiate from page locators.

978-0-595-38677-2
0-595-38677-6